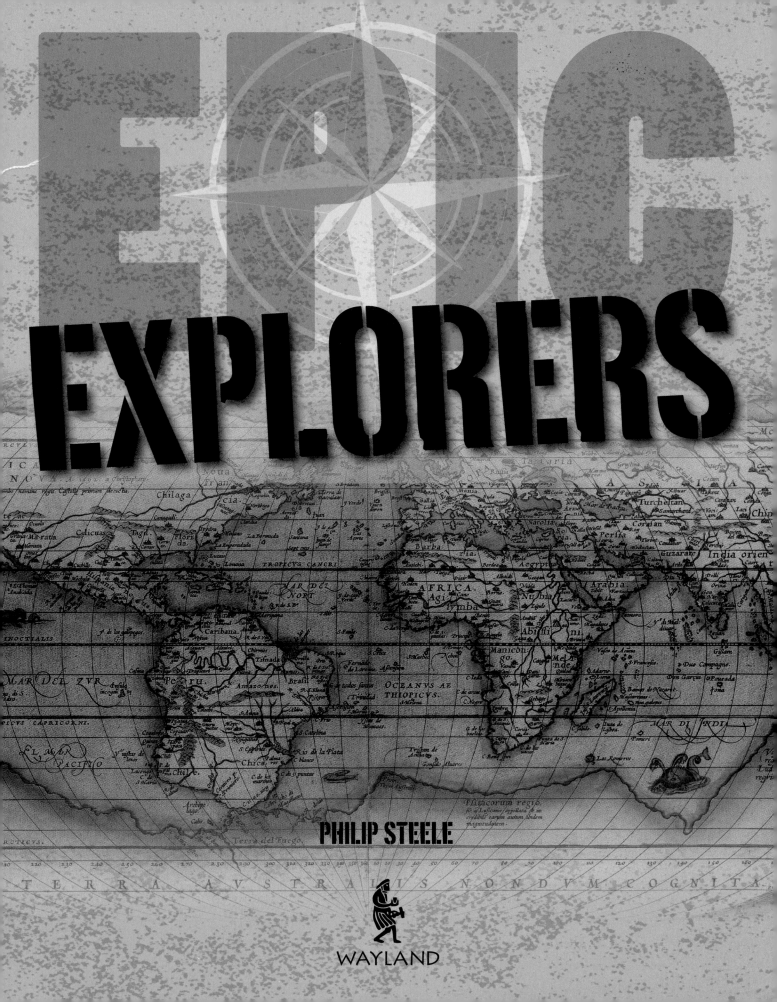

EPIC
EXPLORERS

PHILIP STEELE

WAYLAND

CONTENTS

MARCO POLO

CHALLENGER DEEP

ZHENG HE

JAMES COOK

SCOTT AND AMUNDSEN

INTRODUCTION

Throughout history, people have explored uncharted territory to discover new routes, conquer strange lands and claim amazing wealth.

Driven by a desire to explore the unknown, expeditions have travelled across scorching deserts, dense jungles, frozen ice sheets and the open ocean. They have also gone in search of lost kingdoms, trade opportunities with distant civilisations or just what is over the next mountain.

Other, more sinister, reasons have also pushed people to seek out new regions. The lure of fabulous wealth and the desire to claim new lands, even if people are already living there, have led to a great deal of violence and bloodshed.

WE HAVE MAPPED THE SURFACE OF MARS IN MORE DETAIL THAN THE OCEAN FLOOR.

The history of exploration can be seen in how maps of the world have developed. As more of the surface was explored, so maps became more accurate. This map from about 1570 shows many of the continents as we recognise them today. But it also features inaccuracies, such as an enormous southern continent stretching north into the Pacific and large blank areas across the whole of North America.

Millions of indigenous people have been displaced, enslaved or brutally murdered as other cultures explore and then claim their lands.

With all of the Earth's land surface now mapped and explored, new challenges lie elsewhere. These include diving down to study the ocean's depths, or even blasting clear of Earth's atmosphere to explore outer space and visit new worlds. While the technology may change, the risks for today's explorers remain as high as ever. These new targets of exploration, whether it is the crushing ocean depths or the freezing vacuum of space, are just as dangerous as the vast wastelands were to explorers more than 500 years ago. But that still doesn't stop people from wanting to see what is around the corner, or just over the horizon...

Early explorers told all sorts of fake stories either to claim they had been somewhere where they hadn't, or to make their tales more exciting. Some people even think that Marco Polo made up more than half of his famous China stories!

VIKING EXPLORERS REACHED NORTH AMERICA AS EARLY AS 1000 CE.

HATSHEPSUT

VOYAGE TO THE LAND OF PUNT

Sponsor	Queen Hatshepsut of Egypt
Traveller	Nehsi, Chancellor of Egypt
Route	Saww to Punt
Date of voyage	Summer 1493 BCE
Total distance	about 2,500 km (1,550 miles)

For the ancient Egyptians, the land of Punt was a faraway realm rich in precious metals, woods, spices and resins.

During the 15th century BCE, the Egyptian ruler, or pharaoh, was a woman called Hatshepsut. She instructed her Chancellor, a man from Nubia called Nehsi, to lead an expedition along the Red Sea to Punt to trade in these luxurious items.

The expedition set off along the Egyptian coast in five ocean-going ships that were built of cedarwood and powered by oars and a single, rectangular sail. This was not the biggest Egyptian expedition to Punt, as early records show missions with more than 3,500 men. However, it is the most accurately recorded.

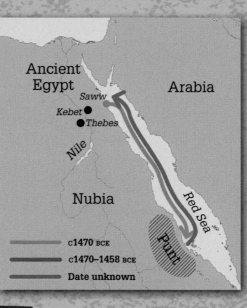

Ancient Egypt · Arabia · Saww · Kebet · Thebes · Nile · Nubia · Red Sea · Punt

c1470 BCE
c1470–1458 BCE
Date unknown

Hatshepsut was one of the most remarkable rulers of Egypt. She was the first ever woman to reign as pharaoh in her own right. Statues show her wearing a false beard because the pharaoh was always portrayed as a man.

TIMELINE

c1479–1473 BCE

In about 1479 BCE, the new pharaoh Thutmose III is only a baby, so Hatshepsut is made regent. In 1473 BCE, Hatshepsut is crowned as co-ruler, effectively taking power.

c1470 BCE

Hatshepsut's Chancellor, a Nubian called Nehsi, is instructed to lead a major expedition to Punt. Five large ships set sail from the Red Sea port of Saww (now called Mersa Gawasis).

After reaching Punt, the Egyptians successfully traded for the precious cargoes they wanted and returned to Egypt. They were accompanied by several dignitaries from Punt who presented Hatshepsut with some of their country's marvels.

All of these details are recorded on the walls of Hatshepsut's huge temple, built at Deir el-Bahri near Thebes, the ancient Egyptian capital. Wall carvings, such as the one below, show the expedition leaving for Punt, scenes of life in Punt and the expedition returning, loaded down with their precious cargo.

TREASURES

The Egyptians came to the land of Punt for the hides (skins) of giraffes, panthers and cheetahs, which were worn by their priests. They took back live baboons, which were sacred animals to the Egyptians. The Puntites also traded in precious wood and gold as well as frankincense and myrrh – scented resins used to make perfumes.

NO-ONE KNOWS EXACTLY WHERE THE KINGDOM OF PUNT WAS.

The last recorded expedition to Punt occurred nearly 300 years later in the 12th century BCE. It was ordered by the then ruler, Ramesses III. According to an ancient papyrus, it was 'loaded with limitless goods from Egypt' and returned safely.

c1470–1458 BCE

The Punt expedition records details of plants, animals and people. It brings back baboons and myrrh trees.

1458 BCE

Hatshepsut dies after a peaceful and prosperous reign.

MARCO POLO

OVERLAND TO CATHAY

Sponsor	None
Travellers	Nicolo, Maffeo and Marco Polo
Route	Venice to China
Date of voyage	1271–1295
Total distance	about 53,000 km (33,000 miles)

Many Europeans had travelled to Cathay (China) before Marco Polo, but none of them wrote such a detailed account of what life was like in the Far East.

In 1269, two Venetian brothers, Nicolo and Maffeo Polo, returned to Venice after a trading journey to the distant empire of Cathay. They carried a letter from the Mongol ruler, Kublai Khan, for the Pope in Rome.

Two years later, in 1271, they went back to Cathay, but this time, they took with them Nicolo's 17-year-old son Marco. They sailed to Acre and then travelled overland through Persia (Iran) to China. They were welcomed by the emperor, Kublai Khan, and Marco worked for him as an official, travelling all over the empire.

Venice · Constantinople · Black Sea · Trebizond · Caspian Sea · Mediterranean Sea · Acre · Jerusalem · Persia (Iran) · Kerman · AFRICA · ARABIA · Gulf of Aden · Indian

In 1298, following his return to Venice, Marco Polo was captured during a war between Venice and Genoa. While he was in prison, he told the amazing story of his travels to a cellmate, who noted them down. These fantastic tales were published in a book called *Book of the Marvels of the World*.

TIMELINE

1269–1271

In 1269, Nicolo and Maffeo Polo return from their first trip to China, with a message for the Pope. In 1271, the merchants set out on a second journey, with 17-year-old Marco.

1271–1275

The Polos cross Persia and Central Asia, following the trading routes known as the Silk Road. After three-and-a-half years, the Polos reach the royal court at Shangdu and are made welcome.

Kublai Khan valued the Polos so much that he would not give them permission to leave his court. This worried the Venetian explorers. They were concerned that, if Kublai Khan died, his successors might not treat them so well.

In 1292, they escorted a Mongol princess to Persia, by sea. The princess was to marry a local ruler and the Polos took the opportunity to return to Venice, via the Black Sea. They arrived at their home city laden with jewels and tales of the mysterious land to the east.

―――――	1269–1271
―――――	1271–1275
――――――	1275–1292
――――――	1292–1295

Kashgar

Shangdu   Cambaluc (Beijing)

Lanzhou●

Cathay (China)

Yunnan

Amoy (Xiamen)

India

Bay of Bengal

South China Sea

Ocean

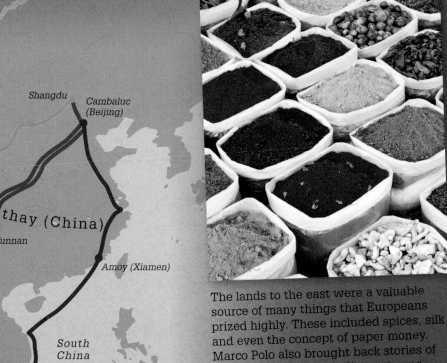

The lands to the east were a valuable source of many things that Europeans prized highly. These included spices, silk and even the concept of paper money. Marco Polo also brought back stories of amazing animals, including unicorns, which were really Asian rhinos.

THE POLOS WERE AWAY FOR 24 YEARS.

1275–1292

Marco Polo travels all over China, Tibet and Burma as an official of Kublai Khan.

1292–1295

Marco Polo's book went on to inspire other explorers. Christopher Columbus had a copy, which is covered with Columbus's hand-written notes.

ZHENG HE

THE GREAT CHINESE VOYAGES

Sponsor	the Yongle emperor
Traveller	Admiral Zheng He
Route	China to Southeast Asia, South Asia, Persia (Iran), Arabia and East Africa
Date of voyages	1405–1433
Total distance	about 169,450 km (105,000 miles)

In 1405, a vast fleet sailed from China on the orders of the Yongle emperor. Its purpose was to impress the peoples of Asia and Africa and develop trade links with them.

The fleet was made up of huge treasure ships, the largest in the world at the time, as well as smaller ships carrying troops, horses and supplies.

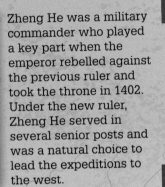

Zheng He was a military commander who played a key part when the emperor rebelled against the previous ruler and took the throne in 1402. Under the new ruler, Zheng He served in several senior posts and was a natural choice to lead the expeditions to the west.

Nanjing

China

Suzhou

Hormuz

Jeddah · ARABIA

Bangladesh
Chittagong

India

Thailand

Dhofar

Arabian
Sea

Mukalla
Aden

Bay of
Bengal

Ayutthaya

Qui Nhon

South
China
Sea

Cochin

Somalia

Sri
Lanka

Semudera

AFRICA

Maldives

Galle

Malacca

Mogadishu
Kenya   Baraawe

Indian

Ocean

Palembang

Indonesia

Mombasa

1405–1411
1413–1422
1424–1433

Java
Surabaya

TIMELINE

1405–1411

The first expedition sails from Suzhou in 1405. The crew make maps and take readings of the stars. The first three expeditions visit Southeast Asia, Sri Lanka, India and Thailand.

1413–1422

The fourth, fifth and sixth voyages go as far as the Maldives, Yemen, Somalia and Kenya. In 2011 and in 2013, remains of medieval Chinese ships were found off the coast of Kenya.

The commander was called Zheng He. He was a Muslim from Yunnan, and he was also a brilliant seafarer. This was just the first of his seven epic voyages.

These journeys took Zheng He and his fleet around Southeast Asia and into the Indian Ocean, visiting Sri Lanka and India before crossing the Arabian Sea to Arabia and the east coast of Africa. During these expeditions, he fought and defeated pirates, impressed local peoples with his diplomacy (and the occasional show of military strength) and traded Chinese luxuries and goods for local animals and produce.

Zheng He died during the seventh and final grand voyage. There is a tomb for him in China, but it is empty because his body was buried at sea.

INNOVATIONS

Chinese sailing technology was more advanced than that of other civilisations. Chinese navigators could use magnetic compasses to find the right direction, rudders to steer the correct course, multiple masts and fore-and-aft rigs to catch enough wind, and bulkheads (watertight compartments in the hull) to keep their ships afloat.

ZHENG HE CONTACTED OVER 30 KINGDOMS.

Some of Zheng He's ships (white) were five times the size of those sailed by Christopher Columbus (orange). The biggest was 137 m (450 ft) long and 55 m (180 ft) wide, with a capacity of 2,540 tonnes. Every ship had two iron anchors, each weighing more than 450 kg (990 lb).

A giraffe was brought all the way back to China, along with zebras, lions and ostriches. Zheng He gave gifts of jewels and gold to local rulers and traded in silk and porcelain.

THE FIRST FLEET CONTAINED 317 SHIPS AND 28,870 CREW.

1424–1433

In 1424, Zheng He set off on the voyage once more. The last great expedition set out in 1430. Zheng He probably died at sea in 1433. His voyages have made China powerful and wealthy.

DIAS & DA GAMA

AROUND THE CAPE OF GOOD HOPE

Sponsor	King John II
Traveller	Bartolomeu Dias
Route	Portugal to South Africa
Date of voyage	1487–1488
Total distance	about 25,600 km (16,000 miles)

Sponsor	King Manuel I
Traveller	Vasco da Gama
Route	Portugal to India
Date of voyage	1498–1499
Total distance	about 38,600 km (24,000 miles)

A great age of European exploration began in Portugal in the 1480s. Two of this nation's greatest seafarers were Bartolomeu Dias and Vasco da Gama.

Trade with India was very important to European countries during this period as the region was a source of exotic materials and spices. However, the land route was controlled by Muslim traders, so the European nations, including Portugal, looked for a sea route to the east that went around Africa.

In 1487, Dias sailed south from Lisbon. His three ships rounded West Africa and reached Mossel Bay, South Africa – but his crew would go no further and he was forced to turn home.

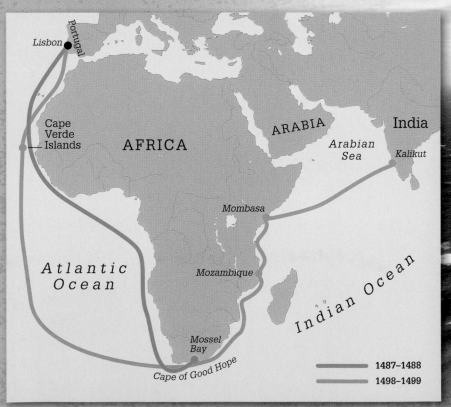

KING JOHN II OF PORTUGAL CALLED THE TIP OF AFRICA THE CAPE OF GOOD HOPE.

TIMELINE

1487–1488

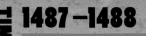

Bartolomeu Dias is sent by King John II of Portugal to seek a trade route to India by sea. Dias sails down the coast

ONLY 54 SAILORS OUT OF 170 SURVIVED DA GAMA'S FIRST VOYAGE.

The caravel was the type of ship used by Portuguese explorers such as Bartolomeu Dias. It had little cargo room, but it was quick and could travel up rivers. Naos or carracks were special ships that were designed by Dias for Vasco da Gama's expedition. They had more space but were slower.

Vasco da Gama's 1498 expedition pushed on around the southern tip of Africa (main image) to Mozambique and Mombasa, before crossing the Arabian Sea to reach Kalikut, India. He was the first European to find a sea route to India.

The new European explorers were not just searching for trade but for control of land and resources. Portugal sent further armed fleets into the Indian Ocean. The fourth voyage was again commanded by da Gama, who treated local peoples with brutality and cruelty.

TREASURES

India was a source of many luxuries, including ivory and pearls for jewellery, ebony for furniture, and indigo to dye cloth. It was also a source of exotic spices, such as pepper, cloves, cinnamon, nutmeg and ginger, which were used to flavour food.

1498–1499

of Africa, but turns back. On the return leg he discovers the Cape of Good Hope.

Dias accompanies da Gama on a new expedition, but only as far as the Cape Verde Islands. Vasco da Gama reaches East Africa and crosses the Indian Ocean to Kalikut.

1500–1524

Dias joins another expedition to India. It discovers Brazil, but Dias dies in a storm off the Cape. Da Gama sails again to India in 1502 and 1524. He is appointed viceroy, but dies of malaria in Cochin in 1524.

COLUMBUS

THE NEW WORLD VOYAGES

Sponsor	King Ferdinand II of Aragon and Queen Isabella of Castile (Spain)
Traveller	Christopher Columbus
Route	Spain to the Americas
Date of first voyage	1492–1493
Total distance	about 14,450 km (9,000 miles)

Convinced that China and the East Indies could be reached by sailing west, Spain commissioned an Italian explorer called Christopher Columbus to find a route.

He set sail across the Atlantic Ocean on 3 August 1492, but had to spend several weeks at sea before he spotted land.

Columbus sailed to many Caribbean islands as well as the coasts of South and Central America. Together, these coasts became known as the 'Spanish Main'.

NORTH AMERICA

Atlantic

- 1492–1493
- 1493–1496
- 1498–1500
- 1502–1506

Bahamas

Cuba

Jamaica

Hispaniola

Trinidad

Pacific Ocean

SOUTH AMERICA

COLUMBUS FIRST WENT TO SEA AGED JUST 13.

TIMELINE

1492–1493
Columbus sails from Palos de la Frontera with three ships, the *Santa María*, the *Pinta* and the *Niña*. He lands in the Bahamas and goes on to explore Cuba and Hispaniola.

1493–1496
The second voyage, with 17 ships and 1,200 men, explores and colonises the Caribbean.

1498–1500
A third voyage explores the coast of South America. On his return, Columbus is arrested and imprisoned.

Christopher Columbus reached land on 12 October 1492. He named the island San Salvador. As well as visiting other Caribbean islands, he established a settlement called La Navidad, leaving behind a group of 39 sailors from the *Santa Maria*, which had sunk in a storm.

Ocean

Azores

Portugal

Spain

Palos
Cadiz

Madeira

Canary Islands

AFRICA

Cape Verde Islands

On 12 October, Columbus and his sailors set foot on land on what is now part of the Bahamas. But Columbus was convinced that he had landed in the East Indies and called all the indigenous peoples he came across 'Indians'. He even thought that the island of Cuba was Japan.

Columbus returned to Spain in March 1493, and was rewarded with great wealth and the title of 'Admiral of the Ocean Sea and Governor of the Indies'. But he remained convinced that he had found a route to the East Indies and he made another three voyages to the region from 1493–1496, 1498–1500 and 1502–1504. During these, he explored more of the islands and coastline and even landed on the mainland of South America.

THE SAILORS LEFT BEHIND AFTER THE FIRST VOYAGE WERE ALL DEAD BY THE TIME COLUMBUS RETURNED.

1502–1506

Once free, Columbus goes on a fourth voyage. He explores Central America and hurricanes strand him in Jamaica. After chronic bouts of illness, Columbus dies in Valladolid, Spain, aged 54.

NEW WONDERS

Spanish sailors and colonists really did find that a new world awaited them across the Atlantic Ocean. There were foods and plants they had never seen before, including maize (sweetcorn), pumpkins, turkeys, pineapples, tomatoes and chilli peppers. There were brilliantly coloured hummingbirds and parrots, and giant lizards called iguanas. Columbus mistook swimming mammals called manatees for mermaids!

MAGELLAN

Sponsor	Charles V, Holy Roman Emperor (also known as Charles I of Spain)
Traveller	Ferdinand Magellan
Route	Around the world from Spain, via the Atlantic, Pacific and Indian Oceans
Date of voyage	1519–1522
Total distance	about 60,440 km (37,500 miles)

While Columbus had failed to find a route to China and the East Indies, many people were still convinced that it was possible to reach these rich lands by sailing west.

The Portuguese navigator Ferdinand Magellan persuaded King Charles I of Spain to fund an expedition to find such a route and he set off in 1519 with five ships and 237 men.

THE CREW HAD TO EAT RATS AND MAGGOT-FILLED BISCUITS!

NORTH AMERICA

Atlantic Ocean

Pacific Ocean

Sanlúcar

Spa

Canary Islands

Cape Verde Islands

SOUTH AMERICA

Strait of Magellan

After the storms the expedition faced in the South Atlantic and sailing through the Strait of Magellan, the sailors found the new ocean to be calm and peaceful. Magellan called it 'Pacific' to reflect this.

TIMELINE

1512–1519

Portuguese seafarer Magellan plans the route, and the Spanish king agrees to finance the voyage. The expedition sets sail from Spain and crosses the Atlantic Ocean to Brazil.

1520–1521

Magellan discovers the strait which bears his name and finds a passage through in 38 days. The expedition crosses the Pacific, landing in Guam.

The *Vittoria* (right) was the only one of the five original ships to make it back to Spain. Of the other ships, the *Trinidad*, the *Concepcion* and the *Santiago* were wrecked or scuttled, while the crew of the *San Antonio* deserted.

Magellan had to sail very far south before he found the Strait of Magellan and entered the Pacific Ocean. However, the expedition was troubled from the start and one crew deserted with their ship before they even reached the Pacific.

The remaining ships took nearly four months to cross the huge ocean. During the crossing, food ran very short and the sailors had to endure terrible conditions.

Having crossed the Pacific Ocean and reached the Philippines, Magellan was caught up in a war and speared to death on Mactan Island on 27 April 1521. It was Juan Sebastián de Elcano, captain of the *Vittoria*, who took over the leadership and led the expedition home in 1522.

Despite the success of the mission, the feat was not repeated for more than 50 years, when the English sailor Francis Drake led the next expedition to sail around the world in 1577.

Many elements of the natural world were named after Magellan. They include the Strait of Magellan, the Magellanic Clouds, Magellanic penguins and galaxies that are found in the southern sky.

1512–1519
1520–1521
1521–1522

Pacific Ocean

Philippines
Mactan
Guam

AFRICA

Indian Ocean

Timor

Cape of Good Hope

Southern Ocean

FEAST AND FAMINE

Off the coast of Brazil, the crew could feast on sweet potatoes, pineapple, sugar cane and the meat of the tapir, which tasted like beef. Later in the voyage, however, food ran desperately short and many crew members died, mostly from scurvy – a disease caused by a lack of vitamin C, which is found in fresh fruit.

1521–1522

Ferdinand Magellan and 40 crew members are killed during a battle in the Philippines. The expedition continues eastwards, stocking up on spices. Only one out of the original five ships returns from the voyage.

ONLY 21 MEN OUT OF THE ORIGINAL 237 MADE IT BACK TO SPAIN.

JAMES COOK

MAPPING THE PACIFIC

Sponsor	King George III
Traveller	James Cook
Route	Around the world, the Southern Ocean, the Pacific islands, North America to the Bering Strait
Dates of voyages	1768–1771, 1772–1775, 1776–1780
Total distance (2nd voyage)	112,500 km (70,000 miles)

In three around-the-world voyages, British naval captain James Cook explored new lands, discovered amazing new animals and provided information that was invaluable to the scientific world.

His first voyage was commissioned to study the planet Venus as it moved across the face of the Sun. Scientists of the day wanted to use information from these observations to work out the distance from Earth to the Sun more accurately. Cook's expedition was sent to Tahiti in the Pacific Ocean to study this event.

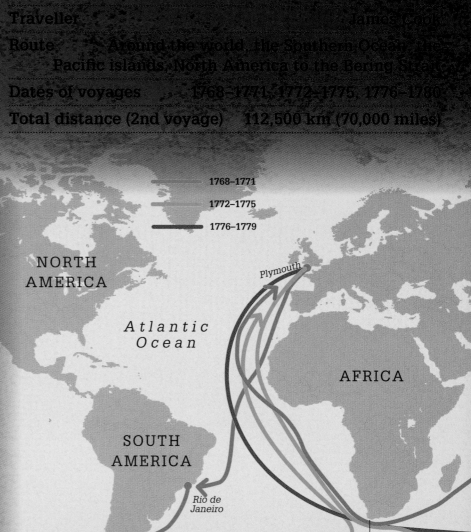

1768–1771
1772–1775
1776–1779

NORTH AMERICA

Plymouth

Atlantic Ocean

AFRICA

SOUTH AMERICA

Rio de Janeiro

Cape of Good Hope

Tierra del Fuego

Southern Ocean

COOK'S SHIP WAS THE FIRST TO SAIL INTO

TIMELINE

1768–1771
Cook sails to Tahiti in HMS *Endeavour* and maps the coast of New Zealand, before landing at Botany Bay, Australia. The ship later runs aground on the Great Barrier Reef.

1772–1775
In HMS *Resolution*, Cook explores the Southern Ocean, crossing the Antarctic Circle. He uses a marine chronometer to assist with navigation, and visits many South Pacific archipelagos.

As part of the voyage, the expedition sailed around and mapped the islands of New Zealand and became the first Europeans to set foot on the east coast of Australia when they landed at Botany Bay. Nearly three years after leaving Britain, the first voyage returned home with tales and discoveries from these new lands.

Cook's second voyage explored the frozen Southern Ocean, searching for a huge island that many scientists believed existed there. The third voyage took him north to Hawaii, Oregon and Alaska, searching for a passage to the Atlantic.

During his third voyage, Cook's ship called in at Hawaii to repair some damage. However, a quarrel erupted between the Hawaiian islanders and the Europeans, during which Cook was killed. The expedition continued, but failed to find any northern passage back to the Atlantic.

THE FIRST VOYAGE RETURNED WITH MORE THAN 3,000 PLANT SPECIMENS.

WEIRD AND WONDERFUL

On Captain Cook's first voyage the expedition's naturalists, Joseph Banks and Daniel Solander, collected, described and drew plants and animals. Many plants are named after Banks. The expedition also brought back more than 1,000 animal specimens, including pouched mammals (marsupials), which were unknown in Europe.

Vancouver Island

Hawaii

Pacific   Ocean

Christmas
Islands

Tahiti

Tonga

Cook
Islands

Easter Island

Batavia

Indian
Ocean

Australia

Botany Bay

New Zealand

Tasmania

Southern Ocean

During his first voyage, Cook did not lose a single sailor to scurvy, which was unheard of at the time. Cook made sure that his crew ate a good diet, including fresh fruit and vegetables, which have high levels of vitamin C.

THE ANTARCTIC CIRCLE.

1776–1779

HMS *Resolution* and HMS *Discovery* sail to Hawaii and on to explore the Pacific coast of North America. Captain Cook is attacked and killed during a fight in Hawaii on 14 February 1779.

LEWIS AND CLARK

Sponsor	US government
Travellers	Meriwether Lewis and William Clark
Route	Camp Dubois, Illinois, to the Pacific Ocean
Date of voyage	14 May 1804–23 September 1806
Total distance	11,265 km (7,000 miles)

At the start of the 19th century, the northwest region of North America was largely unknown, with little having been explored and mapped.

The US government had recently bought a huge area of land from France in the Louisiana Purchase of 1803. It decided to commission an expedition to explore and chart this new extension to the country.

The expedition included more than 30 soldiers, guides and interpreters. They set out west in 1804 and began by following the Missouri river with boats and canoes. Other rivers they navigated included the Clearwater, the Snake and the Columbia.

Map labels: 1804–1805 / 1805–1806; Pacific Ocean; Fort Clatsop; Great Falls; Missouri; Fort Mandan; Territory claimed by Spain, the UK, Russia and the United States; Yellowstone river; Mississippi; Louisiana (US 1803); Missouri; Spanish territory; Camp Dubois

The expedition was travelling through lands that were also claimed by Spain. When the Spanish government heard about this, they sent out armed parties to stop them from claiming the lands for the USA. However, the expedition travelled too quickly and was never caught.

TIMELINE

1803–1804

In 1803, the USA more than doubles in size when it purchases Louisiana from France. President Thomas Jefferson orders an expedition to explore the lands to the west.

1804–1805

The expedition members complete training at Camp Dubois in May 1804. The expedition travels up the Missouri river. In September 1804, they enter the Great Plains. A year later they cross the Rockies (main image).

They crossed vast prairies and traversed the snowy Bitterroots, part of the mighty Rockies (main image). They met more than 50 different Indian peoples and claimed new lands for the USA.

The expedition was also commissioned to study the region's plant and animal life and it discovered many new species. In total, they named 122 new animal species, including ermine, bull snake, bobcat and mountain lion, and 179 plant species, such as the prickly pear cactus and the ponderosa pine.

Sacagawea was a woman of the Shoshone people. She joined the expedition with her husband, Toussaint Charbonneau, and helped the explorers communicate with the local Indians.

IN SEPTEMBER 1805, THE EXPEDITION CROSSED THE ROCKIES.

NATURAL HAZARDS

A 270-kg (590-lb) grizzly bear is a terrifying sight, but the expedition's biggest problem involved smaller beasts. Clouds of mosquitoes and biting bugs made the explorers' lives a misery. Other dangers included bitter cold and white-water rapids. Even so, only one expedition member died – and that was from natural causes.

THE JOURNEY BACK TOOK SIX MONTHS.

1805–1806

In October 1805, they reach the Columbia river and build Fort Clatsop near its mouth. The return begins in March 1806. They reach St Louis, Missouri, on 23 September.

LIVINGSTONE, STANLEY & KINGSLEY

THE EXPLORATION OF AFRICA

The doctor	Dr David Livingstone explored Southern and Eastern Africa 1841–1873
The journalist	Henry Morton Stanley explored Central and Eastern Africa 1871–1877
The writer	Mary Kingsley explored West and Central Africa 1893–1895

For centuries, the interior of the African continent had been hidden to the outside world. Forests, mountains, deserts and wild animals had prevented exploration.

Throughout the 19th century, European geographers, writers, explorers, missionaries, colonists and soldiers arrived to explore the continent.

David Livingstone was a Scottish doctor and Christian missionary. He crossed the Kalahari Desert, explored the Zambezi river and spent years searching for the source of the Nile. He campaigned to end the East African slave trade. In 1855, he discovered Victoria Falls (main image), which he named after the British monarch. The following year, he reached the Indian Ocean, becoming the first European to cross the width of southern Africa.

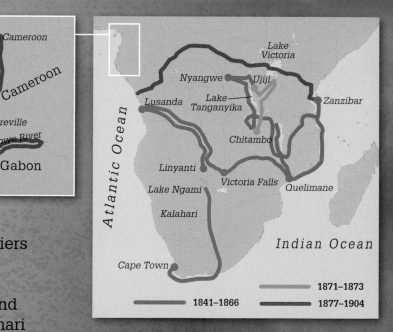

Mt Cameroon — Cameroon — Libreville — Ogowe River — Gabon

Lake Victoria — Nyangwe — Ujiji — Zanzibar — Lusanda — Lake Tanganyika — Chitambo — Linyanti — Victoria Falls — Quelimane — Lake Ngami — Kalahari — Atlantic Ocean — Indian Ocean — Cape Town

1871–1873
1841–1866
1877–1904

STANLEY'S EXPEDITION STARTED WITH 356 PEOPLE. ONLY 114 SURVIVED.

TIMELINE

1841–1866
Scottish missionary David Livingstone arrives in Africa in March 1841. Livingstone's Zambezi expedition starts in 1858. From 1866, he seeks the source of the Nile.

1871–1873
In 1871, Stanley meets Livingstone at Ujiji. Livingstone dies in 1873. His attendants Susi and Chuma carry his body more than 1,600 km (1,000 miles) to the east coast.

1877–1904
In 1877, Stanley reaches the west coast after following the course of the Congo river.

Mary Kingsley, from London, ventured where few European women had dared to go before. She canoed up the Ogowe river in what is now Gabon, collected new specimens of fish and climbed up Mount Cameroon. She died working as a nurse during the Boer War in South Africa in 1900.

Henry Morton Stanley was a Welsh-born journalist who was sent to find Livingstone's expedition, which had gone missing. Stanley tracked the doctor down to Ujiji, by Lake Tanganyika, greeting him with the words 'Doctor Livingstone, I presume'. Stanley then travelled down the Congo, taking 999 days to reach the sea.

Mary Kingsley was an English writer who decided to explore Africa at a time when exploration was not seen as a suitable occupation for a woman. Starting on the west coast of Africa, she learnt survival skills from the local people.

Livingstone suffered from health problems during the final years of his life and he died in May 1873. His heart was buried beneath a Mvula tree in Africa, while the rest of his body was buried in Westminster Abbey, London.

From 1893, Mary Kingsley pioneers exploration by women, travelling in Gabon.

AFRICAN DANGERS

In 1844, Livingstone was attacked by a lion, and his arm was badly injured. Mary Kingsley encountered a crocodile and a leopard. The dangers for African explorers in the 1800s were many. River journeys might run into sudden rapids or waterfalls. Dysentery, sleeping sickness and malaria were common diseases and warriors or slave traders might attack with spears or guns.

SCOTT AND AMUNDSEN

THE RACE TO THE SOUTH POLE

British expedition	
Traveller	Robert Falcon Scott
Route	Cape Evans to South Pole and back
Date of arrival	17 January 1912
Total distance	2,720 km (1,690 miles)

Norwegian expedition	
Traveller	Roald Amundsen
Route	Bay of Whales to South Pole and back
Date of arrival	14 December 1911
Total distance	2,699 km (1,675 miles)

By the start of the 20th century, the frozen continent of Antarctica and the South Pole was the last great challenge to overland explorers.

In 1911, two expeditions set out across the icy wilderness of Antarctica. The Norwegian expedition was led by Roald Amundsen, a veteran of polar exploration. The British team was led by Robert Scott.

SCOTT WROTE IN HIS DIARY: 'GREAT GOD! THIS IS AN AWFUL PLACE.'

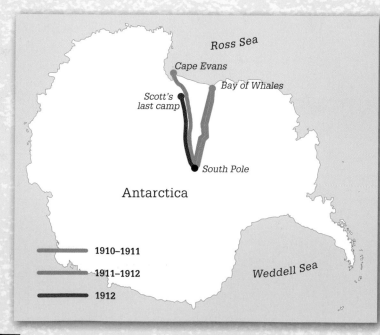

Ross Sea
Cape Evans
Bay of Whales
Scott's last camp
South Pole
Antarctica
Weddell Sea

— 1910–1911
— 1911–1912
— 1912

Both teams chose different methods to haul their equipment. The Norwegian team used packs of dogs to race across the ice. The British team had motor sleds, ponies and a few dogs, none of which worked well. **In the end, they had to pull their sleds themselves.**

TIMELINE

1910–1911

Scott's ship *Terra Nova* is caught in the pack ice for 20 days. The British establish base camp at Cape Evans, while Amundsen sets up base camp at the Bay of Whales. Both teams organise supply depots.

The Norwegian team consisted of 19 men. Five of them, using skis and dog sleds, set out from the Bay of Whales on 19 October 1911, following the Axel Heiberg glacier. They reached the Pole on 14 December (main image).

The British expedition was far larger, consisting of 65 men. A party of five left from Cape Evans on Ross Island on 1 November 1911. They reached the Pole on 17 January 1912, only to find that Amundsen had beaten them to it. And that was just the start of their problems.

On the return journey, Scott's men ran into nightmarish blizzard conditions. They were exhausted and ill with scurvy and frostbite. Supplies ran out and all five of the party died.

Robert Scott was an officer in the British navy. The 1911 expedition was his second to Antarctica, having led the *Discovery* expedition of 1901–4. Among the team on this expedition was Ernest Shackleton, who went on to lead three polar expeditions.

POLAR HAZARDS

In the interior of Antarctica, temperatures rarely get higher than -20°C (-4°F) in the southern summer, and in winter can drop below -60°C (-76°F). Blizzards can make travel impossible. Deadly crevasses may open up in the ice and the whiteness can dazzle the eyes, causing snow blindness.

1911

The Norwegians start out in October, reaching the South Pole on 14 December. The British leave on 1 November and encounter mechanical problems and blizzards.

1912

On 17 January, Scott's team of five reaches the South Pole. By 25 January, Amundsen is already back at base. On his return journey, Scott runs into appalling weather, and all five explorers perish.

CHALLENGER DEEP

DESCENTS TO THE OCEAN DEPTHS

The *Trieste* expedition

Crew	Jacques Piccard and Don Walsh
Date	23 January 1960
Depth	10,916 metres (35,814 ft)

The *Deepsea Challenger* expedition

Crew	James Cameron
Date	26 March 2012
Depth	10,898 metres (35,755 ft)

Even though the seas and oceans cover more than 70 per cent of Earth's surface, they are still one of the least explored regions on the planet.

In the 1870s, HMS *Challenger* surveyed the Mariana Trench in the Pacific Ocean. This British ship gave its name to the deepest place on the planet – a part of the trench that is now called Challenger Deep.

Challenger Deep lies at the southern end of the Mariana Trench. The trench is a deep gash in Earth's crust. It is made by one of the planet's massive tectonic plates being pushed below the surface by another as the two slam into each other.

China

Pacific Ocean

1959–1960

Philippines

Mariana Trench

Challenger Deep

Indonesia

Papua New Guinea

SUBMERSIBLES ARE BUILT TO WITHSTAND THE HUGE PRESSURES AT THE BOTTOM OF THE OCEAN.

1953–1958

The bathyscaphe *Trieste*, designed by Swiss scientist Auguste Piccard, is launched in Italy in 1953. In 1958, it is sold to the US Navy.

1959–1960

Trieste takes part in Project Nekton, a series of deep dives in the Mariana Trench. Don Walsh and Jacques Piccard (son of Auguste) take *Trieste* to the bottom of Challenger Deep.

In 1960, a strange-looking vessel called a bathyscaphe was brought to the Mariana Trench. The *Trieste* had been designed, built and adapted in Europe, but was in the service of the US Navy. Its descent to the ocean floor took nearly five hours, and after 20 minutes on the bottom it took 3 hours 15 minutes to return to the surface (main image).

It was another 50 years before the next successful manned expedition reached this deepest point in the ocean. In 2012, Canadian film director James Cameron became the first person to make a solo descent in a submersible called *Deepsea Challenger*. He spent 2 hours 34 minutes exploring the seabed.

A bathyscaphe is a deep-sea exploration vessel that can move independently and does not need to be attached by a line to the surface. This image shows the *Trieste* being lowered into the water. The ball-shaped part at the bottom is the gondola where the crew sit.

OTHER DESCENTS INCLUDE TWO UNMANNED EXPEDITIONS IN 1995 AND 2009.

2012

Canadian film director James Cameron successfully undertakes a solo descent in *Deepsea Challenger*.

DISCOVERIES

The abyss lies in perpetual cold and darkness. Less remote ocean trenches teem with all sorts of strange creatures, but in Challenger Deep the life forms are small and jelly-like. Microbiologists are fascinated by the microbes – single-celled organisms in the sediment and rocks.

APOLLO 11

EXPEDITION TO THE MOON

Crew	Neil Armstrong, Michael Collins, Edwin 'Buzz' Aldrin
Route	Earth orbit and to the Moon
Date	16 July–24 July 1969
Total distance	1,535,000 km (953,800 miles)

Exploring the vacuum of space beyond the borders of Earth's atmosphere requires a huge amount of effort, courage and technological innovation.

The space race of the 1950s and 1960s saw the two super-powers of the day, the Soviet Union and the USA, locked in a competition of firsts. The Soviet Union had been the first to send a satellite into space and a human into orbit. The USA was determined to be the first to send people to the Moon.

The Apollo missions were America's solution to reaching the Moon and returning. After several test flights, including one that orbited around the Moon, Apollo 11 was to be the first mission to actually land people on the surface. On board were astronauts Neil Armstrong, Buzz Aldrin and Michael Collins.

CM and SM separate — 16 July 1969

20 July 1969

CM re-enters Earth's atmosphere

Florida

Splashdown

Pacific Ocean

The Apollo Moon missions were blasted into space on top of the enormous Saturn V rocket – the tallest rocket ever built (left). Its design was overseen by Wernher von Braun, a German rocket scientist who had built the V2 rockets used during the final months of World War II.

TIMELINE

1957–1961

In 1957, the Soviet Union launches the *Sputnik* satellite. In 1961, Yuri Gagarin becomes the first person in space, and US President John F Kennedy calls for a manned mission to the Moon by the end of the decade.

16 JULY 1969

Launch of Apollo 11.

20 JULY 1969

600 MILLION PEOPLE WATCHED THE MOON LANDING LIVE ON TV.

On 16 July 1969, the mission blasted off from the Kennedy Space Center, Florida, USA. After four days, the astronauts reached the Moon and Aldrin and Armstrong travelled down to the surface, while Collins stayed in orbit. At 2:56 on 21 July 1969, Neil Armstrong became the first person to set foot on the Moon, saying 'One small step for [a] man, one giant leap for mankind'. All three returned safely, splashing down in the Pacific Ocean on 24 July. The whole mission had lasted 195 hours, 18 minutes and 35 seconds.

21 July 1969

24 July 1969

LM docks with CSM

CSM and LM undock

CSM and LM separate.

Landing

CSM orbits moon for 4 days

LM descent orbit

The two astronauts spent about two-and-a-half hours outside their spacecraft on the Moon's surface. They collected 21.5 kg (47.4 lb) of Moon rock to bring home to Earth, set up equipment to study the Moon and planted a US flag.

APOLLO SPACECRAFT

The Apollo Moon missions consisted of three spacecraft. The astronauts travelled to and from the Moon inside the Command Module (CM), which was attached to the Service Module (SM). When they were ready to land on the Moon, two of the astronauts entered the Lunar Module (LM).

21 JULY 1969   24 JULY 1969

exploring the surface of the Moon.

The Lunar Module lifts off from the Moon and docks with the Command and Service Modules (CSM).

A further six Apollo missions were launched, but only 12 astronauts walked on the Moon's surface. An explosion on board Apollo 13 meant that their landing was cancelled as the astronauts battled to bring the spacecraft safely back to Earth.

HALL OF FAME

LEIF ERIKSSON

The son of the famous explorer and outlaw Erik the Red, Leif Eriksson was born in Iceland around 970 CE but probably grew up in Greenland. Sailing west from his home, Eriksson discovered the north-western coast of North America, becoming the first European to set foot on this continent, nearly 500 years before Columbus.

IBN BATTUTA

During the first half of the 14th century, Ibn Battuta travelled across the whole of the Islamic world, from Moorish Spain to India, China, Vietnam and the Philippines.

SAMUEL DE CHAMPLAIN

A soldier and geographer, de Champlain established the first French settlements in North America at the start of the 17th century. He explored and mapped the region around the St Lawrence River and the Great Lakes.

ABEL TASMAN

On a series of voyages in the Pacific from 1642 to 1644, the Dutch explorer became the first European to reach Tasmania (which was named after him) and New Zealand, and to spot the islands of Fiji.

LOUIS-ANTOINE DE BOUGAINVILLE

This French explorer was given command of the country's first official expedition into the Pacific Ocean, which set sail in 1766. He also established the first settlements on the Falkland Islands and almost claimed Australia for France, but was prevented by stormy seas.

ALEXANDER VON HUMBOLDT

Travelling extensively through Central and South America in the early 19th century, this Prussian explorer and naturalist studied the plant and animal life and geology in detail.

SAMUEL & FLORENCE BAKER

This British couple are best-known for their exploration of the central African region around the Nile in the middle of the 19th century, and the discovery of Lake Albert, which was named after the husband of Queen Victoria.

SIR RICHARD BURTON & JOHN HANNING SPEKE

Best known for their exploration of central Africa, this pair of British explorers searched for the source of the Nile. In doing so, they were the first Europeans to visit the African Great Lakes, including lakes Victoria, Tanganyika and Malawi.

NIKOLAY PRZHEVALSKY

This Russian geographer travelled extensively through Central Asia, including northern Tibet and parts of China that were unknown in the West. He also described the only species of wild horse, which now bears his name.

FRIDTJOF NANSEN

A Norwegian explorer, scientist, diplomat and winner of the Nobel Peace Prize, Nansen also led the first expedition to cross the interior of Greenland in 1888.

GLOSSARY

ARCHIPELAGO
A group of islands.

BATHYSCAPHE
A free-moving deep-sea exploration vessel that can move using its own power.

BULKHEAD
A wall inside the hull of a plane or ship, which is designed to strengthen the vehicle and, in the case of a ship, to create watertight compartments.

CARAVEL
A type of sailing ship designed in the 15th century. It was small and very manoeuvrable.

CARGO
The goods carried by a ship or aircraft.

CARRACK
Designed in the 15th century to sail in the Atlantic, this was a sailing ship with three or four masts.

CHANCELLOR
A high-ranking government official.

CHRONOMETER
A very accurate type of clock that was originally developed to help with navigation.

CIRCUMNAVIGATION
A voyage around an island, a continent or the whole world.

DIGNITARY
Someone of high rank.

EAST INDIES
A collective term used to describe the countries and lands of Southeast Asia as well as modern India, Pakistan and Burma.

FROSTBITE
Damage to body parts caused by the cold. Left untreated, skin can turn black, become infected with gangrene and the body part can drop off.

HORIZON
The visible line that divides the sky from the land or sea.

MISSIONARY
A religious person who travels to an area to teach other people about their religion.

MONGOLS
Groups of nomadic herders and warriors from northern and Central Asia who carved out a huge empire.

NAO
A type of sailing ship that was similar to a carrack.

ORBIT
The path of one body around another, such as the Moon around Earth.

PHARAOH
The name given to the rulers of ancient Egypt.

POPE
The head of the Roman Catholic Church, who lives in the Vatican, in Rome.

RE-ENTER
To go into something again, such as when a spacecraft re-enters Earth's atmosphere during its return to the surface.

SCURVY
A disease caused by a lack of vitamin C.

SILK ROAD
The name given to the trade routes that linked China to Europe.

UNICORN
A mythical, horse-like creature with a long horn on its head.

VICEROY
A high-ranking official who governs a region or country on behalf of a king or queen. Viceroys ruled states that were part of an empire.

INDEX

First published in 2015 by Wayland

Copyright © Wayland 2015

Wayland
338 Euston Road
London NW1 3BH

Wayland Australia
Level 17/207 Kent Street
Sydney NSW 2000

All rights reserved.
Series editor: Elizabeth Brent

Produced by Tall Tree Ltd
Editor: Jon Richards
Designers: Ed Simkins and Jonathan Vipond

Dewey classification: 910.9'22-dc23

ISBN: 978 0 7502 8759 3
ebook – 978 0 7502 8760 9

Printed in Malaysia

Wayland is a division of Hachette
Children's Books, an Hachette UK company.
www.hachette.co.uk

10 9 8 7 6 5 4 3 2 1

Picture credits
Front cover top Shutterstock/My Good Images, Front
cover bl Midodrurmund, Front cover bc Shutterstock,
Front cover br courtesy of NASA, 1, 5t Shutterstock,
4 courtesy of NASA, 6b Dreamstime.com/Arossk, 6-7
Dreamstime.com/Vladimir Korostyshevskiy, 8b
Dreamstime.com/Suronin, 9cr Shutterstock/luckyraccoon,
10c Creative Commons Attribution-Share Alike 2.0
Generic license, 13t Jose Manuel, 13b Shutterstock/
michaeljung, 15t Davepape, 16b Shutterstock/
Vibrant Image Studio, 17c Jan Arkesteijn, 19t
KAVEBEAR, 20-21 Shutterstock/Peter Kunasz, 21tr
Shutterstock/Nejhali, 22-23 Dietmar Temps, 23tl
Julian Felsenburgh, 25t Scewing, 25b Print
Collector/Getty, 26-27 Thomas J. Abercrombie/Getty,
27t courtesy of US Navy, 28-29 all courtesy of NASA

GET EPIC!

Cross the globe on a journey of discovery and learn about some of the greatest events from the natural and human world. Read about the most epic migrations, battles, empires and explorers the world has ever seen.

EPIC ANIMAL MIGRATIONS
12 EPIC JOURNEYS — OVER LAND, SEA AND AIR
CAMILLA DE LA BÉDOYÈRE
9780750287579

EPIC BATTLES
12 EPIC BATTLES — ON LAND, SEA AND IN THE AIR
ROB COLSON
9780750287616

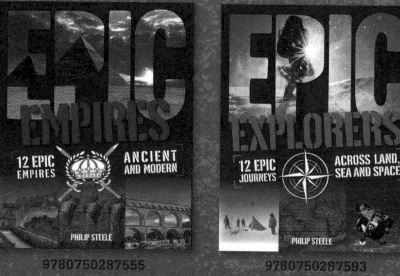

EPIC EMPIRES
12 EPIC EMPIRES — ANCIENT AND MODERN
PHILIP STEELE
9780750287555

EPIC EXPLORERS
12 EPIC JOURNEYS — ACROSS LAND, SEA AND SPACE
PHILIP STEELE
9780750287593